IN BETWEEN

SAIMA

Made with ♥ on the Notion Press Platform
www.notionpress.com

To My Light: Mom and Dad

Contents

Contents

Preface

In Between, a poetry collection that paints myriad shade of growing and trudging swiftly. Our lives are a complete pot of hurdles, warmth and confusion, mixed unevenly. This book present verses that highlight the "in between" spaces of life. Though we see the day and night, there is a midst where we find ourselves stuck. As you read my book, I am abundantly grateful for your every stop and re-visit to pieces of my poetic universe.

Saima

Preface

[illegible]

Acknowledgements

As I send you another bunch of my inner voices, I thank my strongest forces of strength in pushing me to publish them. Mom and Dad, I thank you for being there in my writing journey, showing me every possibility of picking success on every step. I am thankful, and recognise the efforts of my teachers and friends, who never ceased to be my well wishers. *In Between* is a token of appreciation for all those who showed me ways in growing as a poet.

1. Cradling Hope

Halos
Die out
A fog branches in me
I taste pangs
The ones
Which fragment
In scrapped alleys
Sinking blood
Gashes float
Falling
Out of places
Out of love
Out of all
That had once mattered
I grow
Auburn leaves
Of screeching storms
On my scraggy palm
Coiling into death
I rest them
On breaths
Of clogging heart
Maybe
One day closer
To meet eleventh evening

Or to be gone forever
Shelterless
Crackled leaves?
Me?
Our faces
Drenched
More of rain
Wobbling sun rays
We quaver
A scribbled carol
We hold on
It's okay
We will be found
Again

Enter Caption

2. The Moving On Process

Anxiety all over me
Heart clatters
Crackling teeth
The roadways keep fading
How much do I want to hold on?
How much do I long to tarry?
Everytime
I bade farewell to myriad morrows
My head and heart
Had a lasting talk
In between
The memories slipped in
Like deleted hints
That scoop into shadows
No matter how much you walk
They never leave
Coming after you
Coming after doors you shut
Coming after voids you slept in
Coming after strange faces with your name
For once
I want to pause
Stop time to walk into past
"It's hard to move on"
And I still scribble

"Everything has to end"

HOW LONG WILL I STAY?

Enter Caption

3. Silence and Screams

Haul me into waters
Mustard blotches midway
On my scrawny fingers
Like vitiligo's presence
On a dusky face
Sooty freckles on wall bricks
Cluster of chipped sighs
An absent colloquy
Aurelian sand quavers to me
I heard it
When washed out stars
Lurched for bleating rain
Frazzled roof
Sinks
Finds a fleeting home
On dried autumn
Of my shriveling skin
Days flip by
On daubed screen of window
I watch
I wait on
Baked sky
Silver stirred in sapphire
Maybe
An amber summer

Honey on moulding leaves
Or a coral summer
Turning me crimson
In silence
Hands reckless
Bellowing, wailing
Does joy settle for a 'forever'?
Do souring pangs scram away?
My fragments
I gave them to you
Half body
Now I am
Will you come home?
My stenching blood
Smells of longing
Sagacious land
Flaming for breeze
I feel its void
On a day
Aurora
Holds out warmth
Other days
It rips off my only smile
I am stopped dead
Outside flushes
Love,
Restlessly rooting for it
Through cascading petals
Through bustling broadways

In flashes of melting light
In smothered silhouettes at balcony
I am an evening on a day
Laments stumble
I shake
Another hollow opens
I am late again

4. We- Borders

Street lamps
Branching
From bleached white
To warm golden
I wonder
What are we?
Rustic beings
Never ceasing chaos
Always praying for peace
A string left
Untied
In between
Shadows and daylight

Enter Caption

5. We Preach Humanity

Ravaged earth
Half buried lives
Lay forsaken
Terror sits in stones
Frozen after one more blow
Fingers rinsed
Of sand savoring blood
Hatred, Power and Force
Stripped us of
All that we were to be

6. Imagining/ Hallucinating

Distant lullaby
Lumps of mayhem
Greased dawn
Coiling bodies
Stopping by homes
We hallucinate each night

7. Triumph and Fear

I. Sun waves on chinks of smudged mountains. A phantom heart beats on blurred road of my neck. It has gone astray in hopes of catching rainbows. I toss off the grime blanket to faded corner. I am already withering in bits.

II. It is homely for a moment and then melancholy rushes in. The light outside switches from gold to ashes, my barren skin is daubed with mixtures. Divorced dust, cushioning on my shrinking feet; it has tarrying blue silhouettes, so do I.

III. Dusk gales, settling on my empty doorway, there are no traces of any friends. The day long sun is now plunging to a numb land beneath the sandhills, so is the shriveling phantom rhythm on lost roads.

IV. Fatal nights, they always cave in me. I want them to stop blooming someday. Shapeless petals slumber on my skin, the floor cradles my shudders. Walls lock my final sighs, I survived another day, another wrath.

V. I am in between the end of dark and the fringes of light. I feel the triumph of surviving and fear of one more, I wish for it to come then I wish for it to go and then I wish for it to travel through me once more.

8. Still Memories

Pictures
Sheltered in cleaving closet
Some daubed across my bed
Half uttered stories
Hazy sunsets, paused
Haywire of black-brown curls
Hearts rhyming
A similar tune
I get closer
I hear them
In seized moments
I sense life
I feel whole
In lost people
Of unchanged places

Enter Caption

9. Introverted Pages

I. I am at a crossed street. People scramble, faster than wind. I hear their rustling whispers. I do not understand. Do they speak of me? Wondering a sapped petal walking with golden ones. Or do they coax my skin? Dead dust seems to perch on it every autumn. They continue scrambling, I stand still. All at once, the streets feel cold.

II. I am in class. Hoots of laughter seamlessly boom. Then there is a bedlam of voices. Everybody is seeking to tell their yarn of stories. I listen to them, in bits and pieces. I wish to tell my story too. I wish to narrate the sighted mountains and nightfalls at my window. I cannot. I hold on, maybe some other day.

III. I am at the store. The cashier asks me to pay. I rummage for money; a total ruckus. Coins fall, notes lay crushed. I shudder because of unnamed guilt and shame. I hear their uneven snickerings. It amplifies till I turn red. Now I only sense mockery. I glimpse at the person behind me; a scornful disapproval.

IV. I am at a party, joining celebrations of someone's delight. Colors skim by and euphoria multiplies. I sit at an invisible corner. My smile branches as gaiety and melancholy. Can they be felt together? I want to be on the floor too. Something breaks me off. I should be here; rhythmless and aloof.

V. I am in my room. A cave with the safest darkness. I look up. The day replays and night watches it. Why am I this way? A question I always ponder but fail to answer. Silence swells, some questions are better off without answers.

VI. I write. Trying a way to converse. Words brim out. My hands are full of decayed ink and incomplete stories. They spread on scribbled wood, leftover pages and old clothes. I am in search of a new stale place to write the unfinished. Let them stay. I keep locking up what has always been written but never said.

10. Life, Almonds and Storms

I stagger
Far from losing
Life shaped as almonds
Small, brittle and burnt
I keep running
Chasing the city lights
Piling up sorrows
And one day
When I lay
These perfections will die
And my flaws
They will turn one more shade of pale
I will know
I lived life
In storms
And weaved rainbows

Enter Caption

11. Where I Write From

Why do you write so much pain?
And little about hope?
I do not
I write stories
I had held in changing homes
Buried and silenced
Bruised and fragmented
I had lived
All of them
In a cycle
Of shrieks
And a fallen sun

12. A Bygone Friend

I wheel into a hollow
Present looks for courage
She peers into a sealed future
Somedays
I wish for past
Will she ever tell her address?
Does she still live?
I want to stop by
She will hold me close
I will fix myself again

13. My Name is Strength

I feel it
An intensity
Growing beneath my ribs
Leaping out of lungs
Like mountain carpets
Expressing volcanos
Fierce, limitless but powerful
Years of confinement
I will finally end them
Untying the rusts and rot
I will be free

14. Ma: A Being of Stifled Stories

I. I beam at your face, it swims between rootless terror, flickering hope and fading innocence. I touch your dreams, writing farewell letters to no known addresses. The hollows continue eating your eyes. How many more griefs to count till it is all over Ma? The aches keep throbbing but you never stop them.

II. We gaze at the sunset; attending its dusky funeral, together. Ma, does holding onto hope feel the same? Each daybreak, you wake up, battle, crumble and wake up again. Silence seems to never reconcile between us. It has too many questions with unfinished answers. How has life been to you Ma? I wish I could plead this half wilting orange horizon to empty nightmares that sleep beside you all the time. Do your dreams wish the same?

III. I hear you at the stove, smothering screams of your burnt fingers with biting spices. You keep stirring nostalgia in uneven amounts to brew a lamenting future. Autumn flames of slitted kitchen swirl, bellow and die. You kill them, like you did to your ambitions, your words and your voice. These pallid walls cage your heart, it burns to wither and withers only to survive.

IV. The nightfall is finally here Ma and I can tarry closer to you. We peer into each other's faces, searching for one more reason to live life. I want to be your human diary someday, can I be? I will be an anchor and you can put off those dateless years of harbouring burden, agony and decay. As the room coils into a blinding shadow, I sense you growing frozen. You scurry under the ailing moon, as if searching for something lost so untimely. Ma, do you still yearn for a past that never pleaded to stay?

15. Can We Be Strangers Again?

I. I had to get away. Pack my bags and never return to the place we built together. I see demons, replacing you. Each night, the depth grows and the sky shivers. You feel no more like a human, but a dead leaf which flips with every blow.

II. I had to get away. What we had is long gone. Whom do we blame? My silence as I watch you burn. Or your thunder that screamt behind concealed doors. We sit at the edges. I look into your gaze; I see myself homeless. Can we be strangers again? You forget my face; I never ask your name. Maybe then, we will stop painting hurt beneath our pillows each day.

16. My Mirrored Woman

And when this world swallows us
I will meet you again
On the same bridge
Where you clasped my hand
Showed me the woman I am
We will speak
Of all the gales
And tiny moments
We shaped them together
From our backyards
Into our hearts

17. How I Write Pain

Have a cup of lament
Add a pinch of tremor
Lay ink on blank sheets
Your hands will begin
Spirals of words
And rotting phrases
With one pain comes infinite poetry

Enter Caption

18. A Petal's Story

Halfway through life
It decays
Memorialized
In sooty frames
Once
It laid on your hair
Like a treasured piece of love
Marking a smile for stories you read
Then mere footmarks and splatters
How did they change it so much?

Enter Caption

19. A Search Within

All those time
You had scurried
After fogged faces
Looking for home (homes?)
Marked on brittle lanes
There is only one
Far away but close
It lives in you
You are your only home

20. Swelling Between No Ends

We had put faith
In withering
In yellowing dawns
Never swelling beyond skyline
We fluttered
Whispering peace
To cluttered hearts
Smudged moon
Fading to no known addresses
No one loves scars
Can they teach life?
Maybe…yes
Burnt faces
Clutched between
Dust and stale red
We pulled out
From homes having no doors
Untangling mazes
With no bridges
Splattered windows
Plastering
Stories,
We scribbled
We never began

Churning and crumbled
On roads
Fragmenting with no names
In hallways
Reeking of nightmares
We lived all
We survived all
That had no ends

21. One Breath A Day

Summer hearts
Sun soars
Growing on our faces
We are made
Of light and warmth
No darkness
Stayed here
For long
Sorrows
Bind them with gratitude
There is no going back
This day
We will live it each breath

22. In Between Two Worlds

Silence at the door
You perch at stairs
Looking through
Chipped wounds of blinds
Will the knocks
Reach your heart this time?
Dusty books
In it stories
Known to an amnesiac generation
Graze through them
You will find the winds
Asking to uncage
There lives a whole new world
Beyond what has been told

23. Darkening Abuses

My skin is an aged old tale
Of discrimination, loneliness and disgrace
Stifled by generations of history
Every time I peered on faces
A shade of ignorance
Mixed with mockery
Strangers?
Or maybe ashamed to call out my name
I have been a part of celebrations
Lights, laughters and joy
None to celebrate me
I sit close to people
They keep going astray
Piercing the wounds flapping within
I am the dust shutting their eyes
I am an eclipse they seek shelter from
Who am I?
I ask stars for hopelessness
I wish to be a different skin
People will love me then
I wish someone so close to me
Not an inch distance between us
I wish being dark was not an inherited crime
I wish worrying creases leave my mother's face
That she has to not question her womb

My skin is an aged old tale
And my heart
An abandoned tunnel
The same colour as me

MY SKIN IS A TALE OF STIFFLED HISTORY

Enter Caption

24. Close To Be

I kept you a box
Of spiraled poetry
And letters
Half written
With empty words
Read them to me
When I am
Between the sky and sea
And I will tell you
I am closest
To every light
That I craved to be

I AM GROWING IN THE LIGHT I CRAVED

Enter Caption

25. A Promising Address

Your skin wilts
On roads
With no birth dates
But entombed in graves
What do you name days
That hold no sun
Tragic stories?
Poet's cacophonies?
Some lost
Many crumbled
Flashing between
Those eyes
That have only seen
Wars with frozen cities
And skies
Feeding on tears
Still
You wake up
As new dawn breaks
Looking beyond
Every decay and crack
Hope writes your address
On locked doors
You never find it
But it stops by

Here and there
All the time

26. You: A Faithful Galaxy

Chapped wounds
Beneath your skin
Spelling 'pain'
Of all kinds
A self-prisoned tale
Holding onto closed doors
A worm-eaten story
No one keeps it for long?
A demon carving
'YOU ARE BARE EMPTY'
Are you?
You break off
Blown and ashed
Harboring a grey history
With hushed battles
Will this world ever see?
And you grow out
Watching death so closely
In torn autumns
With no light to breathe
You are an infinite galaxy
Where faith never quits

Enter Caption

27. Wars and Wounds

I stand
Dust wears me
A futile shelter
I would be found before sunset
I tell you
This city is dying
Dying (of bustling voices)
Dying (no memories speak)
Dying (time stitched with death)
Nights hardly arrive here
Days split between
Smoke and sun
You keep looking
It is all gray
So little of breaths
So much of haze
I turn pages
Of my diary (my only past)
Like a new light
At the edge of street
It beams
But does not call my name
What if they hear me?
You tell me
We will be back soon

Everything
Will fit in the right places
But
What if there were no right places?
And I tried fitting in shadows
What if I held emptiness?
And raised it as hope all this time
What if there was never a new light?
And I hallucinated its abandonment
You say again
It will be okay
Some day?
And I know
Home will feel so foreign
No new walls
Can replace its name

28. A Futile Merge

This city is me
I walk in
I sense distance
I live on its streets
And sleep on plastered edges
There are no doors
There are people
Do they see me?
Will they hear me?
I have staggered miles now
Asking way out
To blurred faces
They look so much like home
Go close
No feelings
No addresses
This city is me
I am eating its loneliness
And harbouring cries
I watch its hands
Holding a blazing me
Staking bruised hopes
And gliding miseries
This city is me
I continue chanting

I will
A maniac
A desperate body
Till I become one of it
Broken
Breathing
I look into holes
Of its locked heart
Was it there all this time?
I see so much
I see nothing
This city is me
I am this city
We live destruction
We live nowhere
We are nameless

29. A Hypocrites' Bloodline

Why do they preach freedom?
As they wipe it off
Naming it disgrace on our faces
So cage it tight in your hearts
But never let it free
You try it
Once
Twice
Countless
And they say
You are different
In every wrong ways
We scream with night
And whisper into dawn
We do all
To be heard
To just be are ourselves
This is not us
This will never be
Here are wilting mannequins
Murky, lifeless and frozen

30. I and Alien

A pungent growth
Ceaseless
Do you not see it?
Why do you tell me it is all in my head?
Why do you try showing me it is not there?
It is there
It has always been
Shrieking through my cracks
Chasing me out of bed
One step
Two step
So many steps
I cannot count
It is close
It is far
It is everywhere
It reaches out for me
It pulls me in
I see no rays
No walls spellHOPE
My memories quarrel in pieces
When was I happy?
Will you tell me?
I do not remember
It is pacing

Tell me my sane tales
One last time
Two last time
As many times you can
I am becoming a stranger
My mirror forgets my name

31. Living the Midways

I. We put faith in moving on. We walk out to be at peace. We look above and name it a new day. We sit by the window, hoping the winter stories of our hearts will finally rest. We write a new page in our diary, laying *'yesterdays'* in slumber.

II. We hear the demons breaking in. We stumble, we bleed, we are chaotic. We see, call out the sun and choose to never cease. This is us. We are '*in between.*'

Enter Caption

32. A Fleeting Option

And in this town
Where new homes
Come hastening
Camouflaging old ones
There is so much
You can keep
But never take
In shattered songs
And rustic pages
Sun goes down
Once again
Close to waters
Far from skies
One more memory
Locked safe
To be lost
Later and for always
Paper hearts or fragile love?
Whom do you blame?

33. An Unsolved Dilemma

Nights
When your heart stopped?
But you still breathed
Was your heart ever there?
Or
Did it haunt you to live?

34. Faceoff and Victorious

Tomorrow
I will find peace
The holes are healing
Tomorrow
I will call out the sun
It will have no shadows
Tomorrow
I will cross the bridge
This time
Holding my strength
Tomorrow
I will see my mother smile
A bit wider
She is forgetting for good
Tomorrow
I do not need to run
I can be here a little longer
Watch the lights travel
And ashes passing to fade
Tomorrow
I do not have to protect my dreams
I will let them run
Wild, free and fearless
Tomorrow
The day will be bandaging

I will overcome my yesterday
Tomorrow
I can walk past the bleakness
The demons are gone
Or they choose to forget
Tomorrow
I will look into the mirror
See myself
See *hope* after so long

35. Dreaming In Between

I watch myself
Lost between
A harrowing past
A drooping road
My future
Brighter than flames
Illusioning on oceans

36. Illusionary

Circles
Hear the sands
Tossing over my feet
I stumble
I crawl
I cry
I crack open
I see my home
I enter
It tells me
'I live here no more'

37. A Call

Fireflies
Light me up
I am sad
I need a friend
Or myself?

Enter Caption

38. Pieces of You

And we exist
If not in us
Then in people
Let them bloom
In those
We left
We lost

Final Words

Thank You for reaching the end with In Between. As you trace through the farewell, I hope this book reached in different cities, corners and shades of your heart. A final regard before you leave,

"May your light never cease."

Aakhir

The End

Printed by Libri Plureos GmbH in Hamburg,
Germany